Who Is the Beast?

BY KEITH BAKER

Mc Graw Hill **Wright Group**

The **McGraw·Hill** Companies

www.WrightGroup.com

Wright Group

The **McGraw·Hill** Companies

The beast, the beast! We must fly by!

We see his tail swing low and high.

The beast, the beast! I must turn back.

I see his stripes, yellow and black.

The beast, the beast! I buzz along.

I see his legs, sure and strong.

The beast, the beast! Don't make a sound.

I see his eyes, green and round.

The beast, the beast! I hide from sight.

I see his whiskers, long and white.

The beast, the beast! I'm filled with fear.

I see his tracks — the beast is near!

Who is the beast? Who can it be?

I see no beast. I just see me.

Am I the beast? Could the beast be me?

I must go back to them and see.

I see whiskers, long and white.

We both have whiskers, left and right.

I see eyes, green and round.

We both have eyes to look around.

I see legs, sure and strong.

We both can jump far and long.

I see stripes, yellow and black.

We both have stripes across our backs.

I see a tail swing low and high.

Both our tails swing side to side.

Who is the beast? Now I see.

We all are beasts — you and me.